It's just words…
Right?

N.B. Kitten

BookLeaf
Publishing

Presentation by *BookLeaf Publishing*

Web: www.bookleafpub.com

E-mail: info@bookleafpub.com

ISBN: 9789395755177

First edition 2022

DEDICATION

This poetry collection is dedicated to my incredible family who have supported me from start to finish with this project!

Ashley, Dawn and Andy for never letting me give up.

Cole and kara for being the most amazing siblings.

My beautiful daughters for giving me a reason to fight.

Last but not least Miss B Midgley for her input and patience with me while I pulled my hair out putting this together!

ACKNOWLEDGEMENT

Many thanks to Kyle for getting this book rolling, thanks to b kitten for being amazing, thanks to the world for being so shit that I have plenty to write about!

What did I do to deserve this?

What did I do to deserve this?
Where did I go wrong?
You'd think I'd slain 5000
And karma's still going strong
Just as I think I've found peace
Reality slaps me in the face
Just as I think it can't get worse
I'm shown the last was just a taste
A taste of whatever hell Is to come
What disaster is to next knock me down
All out of fight to get back up
Knowing eventually I'll drown
Drown in my thoughts and hopeless dreams
Existing where I clearly don't belong
What did I do to deserve this?
Where did I go wrong?

Time becomes irrelevant

Time becomes irrelevant
When a second feels like an hour
Trapped within a moment
That i can't overpower
Those few seconds after I wake
When reality is distorted
trying to catch my breath again
My thoughts are still contorted
Send me back to dreamland
Where life isn't all consuming
Where my mind isnt working against me
And darkness isn't constantly looming
I wake up again and face the world
For at least one more day
But time becomes irrelevant
When you wish to dream it all away

Hopelessness consumes me

Hopelessness consumes me
And Steals my every thought
Leaving me with not much more
Than broken pieces from battles fought
I glue my pieces back together
After each and every war
Losing shards of myself along the way
Making it so much harder to ignore
How do I put myself back together
When I don't have every part
When I'm drowning in nothing and everything
There's a shadow, where once was my heart
Thought racing fast than I can process
I'm struggling to catch my breath
Suffocated by the empty promises
Of a quiet and peaceful death

I thought that I could do it

I thought that I could do it
But I can't as it turns out
And yet here am still burning
In the fire of self doubt
even though I'm well aware
The damage that I've inflicted
Im still happy to take the pain
As i fall apart, as predicted
Self destruction masterclass
How much can I endure
I reached my limit, I am done
I can't take it anymore
Free me from this misery
Untie me from my pain
Let me slip away quietly
Because this is inhumane

Please someone help me

5

Please someone help me
For I am all alone
Surrounded by my loved ones
Does that make my heart cold stone?
Please someone help me
As tears fall from my eyes
As jokes are told around me
But My sense of humour died
Please someone help me
I feel I can't go on
With so much still to live for
Yet I feel my time is done
Please someone help me
No. Really. I need support
I'm hanging on by a thread
Wishing for a life cut short
Please no one help me
It's too late to be saved
The intrusive thoughts win this time
To their demands, I have caved

Thoughts overwhelm me

Thoughts overwhelm me
Weighing me down
Rocks tied around my ankles
Preparing to drown
Pulling me deeper
no strength to fight
Water filling my lungs
Fast losing light
Thoughts slowing down
Calm washes over me
At last I'm at peace
From my mind I am free

I'm losing my grip on reality

Im Losing my grip on reality
The fog suffocating my mind
Blurring fact and fiction
A truth my thoughts designed
I don't know what is real
No longer able to tell
Is this really happening
Did i find my way to hell
Kept prisoner inside my head
A jail Created by me
Yet still clawing at the walls
I can't set myself free

I've overstayed my welcome

I've overstayed my welcome
Yet I know that I can't leave
A constant sense of unwavering guilt
With no signs of a reprieve
Unwelcome, unwanted, unloved
Silence has never been harsher
Despite the many futile attempts
I'm No closer to my departure
Lonely, empty, misunderstood
The void is getting harder to hide
Fragments at a time, I'm losing myself
My own peace, I can't provide
Because I've overstayed my welcome
Inside of my own head
A war within, against myself
Everything and nothing left unsaid

My mind is whirling

My Minds whirling, twirling, I'm going to explode
I've bottled this up, and carried on down this road
I blinded myself, made sure I couldn't see
I knew i couldn't handle what's right in front of me
So I smiled and I laughed and I tried to ignore
The pain and the grief that hurts to the core
The moments I forget are they worth all the rest?
Worth the pain and hurt, and this whole mess?
When deep down I know I'm only fooling me
To think there could ever be a time to be happy
A few hours alone I come to a conclusion
I try to follow it through, but it's all an illusion
The words refuse to exit my mouth
My exit strategy starts to go south
I can't seem to give up I can't let go
Maybe the moments are worth the low
I'm confused and I'm lost, nowhere to turn
This needs to end, One day I'll learn

Would it be insane?

Would it be insane?
To try to hide from the pain,
the emotional drain,
the heartbeat in my brain,
life's Bane,
hearts stain,
is it insane to need to be normal again?
Abstaining, refraining never regaining
Am I insane?

Darkness

there's a darkness, an emptiness,
 that I cant escape
 creeping over me
 like a blanket, a drape,
 a shadow, a cloud,
 a grave getting deeper
if I said 'I want out'
would that make me any weaker?
than everyone else that is struggling too?
 than everyone else that is muddling through?
 should I be stronger? should I man up?
I don't think I can, this shit just wont stop
 the loneliness is deafening,
the emptiness is cruel,
I feel like i'm being stupid,
I feel such a fool,
 I've got so much to live for,
yet nothing left to lose,
how the fuck does that work?
 I am so confused!
 this crucifying cycle that I cant seem to break
this stupid smile i'm struggling to fake,
my head Is so heavy i'm so fucking tired,
each attempt of happiness, completely backfired,
I hope the end is near,

one way or another,
this will all be over,
 I wont feel so smothered,
 so lost, so empty,
 bruised and broken,
 'And still I rise'
not a truer word spoken!

INTRUSIVE THOUGHTS

Inside my mind, an abomination
Nighttime stirs a confrontation
Two sides, with their own explanation
Rational thoughts at their expiration
Ultimately losing all justification
Shame and guilt on a cruel rotation
I can't handle this situation
Vulnerable, scared and pure frustration
Entering my mind is a self assassination

Thoughts I tried to keep at bay
Hidden struggles I tried to delay
Overthought feelings out on display
Unraveling more and more each day
Giving in to the voices asking me to obey
Hating myself for having been led astray
Trapped in my mind in a hellish relay
So desperately hoping this voice goes away

There's something about you

There's something about you
That draws me
There's something there
That flaws me
There's a way about you
That steals me
Just a way
That heals me
There's something about you
That soothes me
Lifts me up
It moves me
There's a way about you
That sees me
Into my soul
That frees me
There something about you
That warms me
Just a glance
That reforms me
There's something about you
That cures me
Unseen wounds
That endures me
Just something about you

Time to decide

Time to decide
Live life or die?
Give life a chance
Instead of saying 'goodbye'
Your feeling so broken
Beyond all kinds of repair
Feeling nobody listens
Or nobody cares
Feeling so distraught
Hopeless, giving in
Can you turn it around?
Bring calm back within
I know it's not easy
When you've had enough
Think of the positives
That make life less tough
Try and hold on to
One good moment each day
Pass up on the negative
Throw that all away!
It won't ever be a straight path
With all the rises and dips
Times when your climbing
Times when it all slips
In the dark times remember

It won't always remain
Stop hurting you more
Inflicting self pain
I feel you've suffered enough
I know you don't agree
Please take it on board
You're not worthless you see
Nothing is perfect
That does not exist
Ups and downs are so normal
Don't die you'd be missed
You believe no one would notice
If you were to be gone
That belief is ingrained
But so terribly wrong
Let's turn this around
Find a slither of hope
One step at a time
You can learn to cope
Learn to manage the present
And work through the past
It will take some time
You can't do it fast
Just keep striving and smile
One day you'll be free
It won't always be hard
Just being me

I started out with everything

I started out with everything
And slowly lost my way
Piece by piece I disappeared
Parts of myself I gave away
Just small things here and there
Things I thought I wouldn't miss
I ignored myself getting smaller
My doubts I would dismiss
But my empty shell couldn't hold me up
And Finally I came to see
I needed to find my voice again
The only one who could do that was me
Suddenly I'm the bad guy
For protecting the little That remains
I guess I'll take that title
If it means breaking from these chains
If your people aren't happy to see you shine
And to your growth they have objections
They were never your people anyway
And they don't deserve your affections
Keep your pieces, look after them well
Stay true to everything in which you believe
Share your heart, don't give it away
Else one day for that heart, you will grieve

I'm twisted! I'm tense!

18

I'm twisted I'm tense I'm screwed up in a ball
So I grab my pen and wait for words to form
The ink is my relief flowing onto the page
 I start to unfold I release my rage
My hand is moving of its own free will
 I'm ironing out I'm standing still
My new release, this seems safer
Words written down rather than blood on paper
 Than razor on skin, than cutting too deep,
Now I have more than my scars to keep
 So I thank the paper and I thank the pen
And say goodbye to that blade again

Asphyxiation

asphyxiation
like suffocation intoxication
crawling, falling
the abyss
i can't miss
But an echo
from the depths
as a thousand tortured souls caress
intertwine and refine
the inner wolf
interjects
and resurrects
And the fall is the gift
that shifts
the eclipse
and i start to awaken
chart a path
to salvation
All is fine
for a time
but theres a calling I'm ignoring
my addiction
my affliction
that fills the hole in my soul
like an echo

from the depths
and a thousand tortured souls caress
excite and unite
the inner demon
retrieves
and deceives
and
I can't breath
like
asphyxiation,
suffocation intoxication

Go away!

Sometimes I wish they'd go away,
these feelings so intense!
The weight of it's too much to bear,
the weight is too immense.
When I feel, it is no game.
It gets the best of me.
A prisoner of my heart I am
that can never be free.
The fear of going overboard
is always on my mind.
That one day just a note is all
my loved ones are gonna find.
I'm ruled by my emotions.
Governed by my heart.
Inseparable my feelings from
which I cannot part.
What would I be without these chains
bound tightly round my heart?
An animal without the sense
to dread its sorry lot.
Sometimes I wish they'd go away,
these feelings so intense!
The weight of it I have to bear
though the weight is so immense.

Could there ever be a day

Could there ever be a day,
My mind won't lead me astray,
Tell me all that's right is wrong
My brain working against me all along
Is there hope to reach the light
Will there be an end in sight
Or should I just give up this fight
Sink into the darkness of the night
Smiles leaves as quick as they came
I'm too far gone to win this game
My world comes crashing down on me
A mess, a failure, displayed for all to see
I feel the crushing in my chest
I want to die just for the rest
A break from life is all I need
Just a day and I'll be freed
From the shackles of my mind
Grasp at the peace I long to find

I don't know how I got here

I don't know how I got here, Back in this head space
I tried to avoid it so many times, Yet I'm right back at the same place.
I don't want to fail, I don't want to break
I don't want to do something I'll regret, I don't want to make a mistake.
My days are slow, They are painful
I don't know how much time I have, I don't know how to be thankful.
Peaceful sleep never comes any more, Smiles don't brighten my eyes
I feel hopeless and stuck in the lows, Searching for the highs.
No I don't mean drugs, I mean the moments when I breathe
When I'm not stuck, Full of sadness that begins to seethe.
Bright stars I do not gaze, Friends I do not call
Never in my life, Have I ever felt so small.
I can't fix the problems I own,
All the best parts of me, I've seemed to outgrown.
I don't want to gain, I don't want to loose

For all I can do is be still, In life I won't have to
choose.
I'm not okay , I'm not alright
I am tired, I don't want to fight.
"Get up!" I scream inside
But I can not move an inch,
As if I'm stuck in a nightmare, In need of a
pinch.
This is not real, I have to move
Nothing's going to change, Nothing's going to
improve.
All the space of life, The pain begins to take up
I can't stay this way, I have to wake up

Breathing hole

When you finally find a breathing hole
That very first gasp of air
For a second it feels so good to breathe
And you forget you were ever there
When you finally catch a break in the clouds
You're warm and dry and free
For a second you don't remember the storm
Or being trapped in a mountain of debris
When you finally break out of the loop
You're no longer circling the drain
For a moment you don't remember darkness
You remember the warmth of light again
seconds they turn to minutes, hours, days
When suddenly you realise that you won
You kicked depressions fucking Arse
Your life has just begun
Take in the air and feel the warmth
Enjoy and Treasure every day
Smile as often as you can
The warmth is here to stay!

www.ingramcontent.com/pod-product-compliance
Lightning Source LLC
Chambersburg PA
CBHW061324140726
47998CB00007B/2551